BIOENGINEERING IN THE REAL WORLD

by Meg Marquardt

Content Consultant
Eric S. Richardson, PhD
Department of Bioengineering
Rice University

Core Library

An Imprint of Abdo Publishing
abdopublishing.com

abdopublishing.com

Published by Abdo Publishing, a division of ABDO, PO Box 398166, Minneapolis, Minnesota 55439. Copyright © 2016 by Abdo Consulting Group, Inc. International copyrights reserved in all countries. No part of this book may be reproduced in any form without written permission from the publisher. Core Library™ is a trademark and logo of Abdo Publishing.

Printed in the United States of America, North Mankato, Minnesota
082015
012016

Cover Photo: Michael Svoboda/iStockphoto
Interior Photos: Michael Svoboda/iStockphoto, 1; Bettmann/Corbis, 4; Ralph Morse/Life Magazine/Tima & Life Pictures/Getty Images, 7; Red Line Editorial, 9, 39; iStockphoto, 10, 24, 30; Mario Vazquez/Agencia MVT/AFP/Getty Images, 12; MPI/Getty Images, 15; SSPL/Getty Images, 16; John Stillwell/Press Association/AP Images, 20; Elizabeth Hoffmann/iStockphoto, 23; Stocktrek Images/Corbis, 27; Erik de Castro/Reuters/Corbis, 28, 45; George Glew/Rex Features/AP Images, 32; Evan Vucci/AP Images, 35, 43; Allen Breed/AP Images, 36

Editor: Arnold Ringstad
Series Designer: Ryan Gale

Library of Congress Control Number: 2015945538

Cataloging-in-Publication Data
Marquardt, Meg.
 Bioengineering in the real world / Meg Marquardt.
   p. cm. -- (STEM in the real world)
 ISBN 978-1-68078-039-0 (lib. bdg.)
 Includes bibliographical references and index.
 1. Bioengineering--Juvenile literature.   I. Title.
 660.6--dc23

2015945538

CONTENTS

THE HEART OF THE MATTER

By 1969 Haskell Karp had been ill for many years. He had heart problems. He needed a medical miracle to survive. There had been recent heart surgery breakthroughs. But procedures were dangerous. Many patients were dying.

In Texas, Michael E. DeBakey's lab had created an amazing invention. It was an artificial heart made

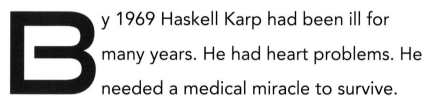

DeBakey's artificial heart contained four chambers and was powered by a machine outside the body.

out of plastic, metal, and other materials. The heart was an achievement of bioengineering. Bioengineers blend biology and engineering. They often create medical devices. DeBakey's artificial heart worked like a real heart.

The artificial heart was only a temporary solution. It kept patients alive while waiting for a real organ to become available. DeBakey's heart had only been tested in animals. The results did not look good. However, Haskell Karp was in dire need. His doctor decided to try it. On April 4, 1969, Denton A. Cooley took out Karp's damaged heart. He placed the artificial heart into Karp's empty chest. It worked. Sadly, Karp died three days

Fighting Over Hearts

The first artificial heart caused a major controversy. The device had not yet been approved for human use. Cooley did not ask permission to use DeBakey's heart. The result was a long feud. Cooley claimed he used the heart to attempt to save a life. But DeBakey believed using an untested product was wrong.

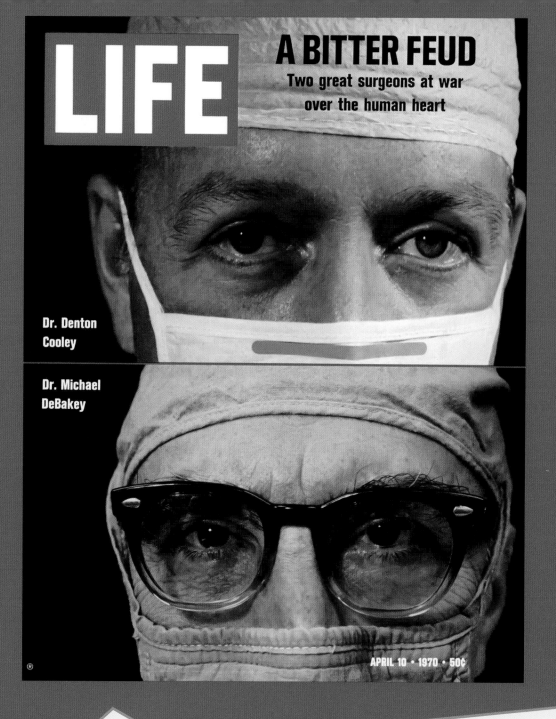

LIFE

A BITTER FEUD
Two great surgeons at war
over the human heart

Dr. Denton
Cooley

Dr. Michael
DeBakey

APRIL 10 • 1970 • 50¢

DeBakey and Cooley became famous for their pioneering work on heart implants, appearing on magazine covers after the historic surgery.

later. But it was an important event in medical history. Today bioengineered solutions are common for heart problems.

Keeping Pace

In the 1950s, pacemakers were introduced. These devices send out electric pulses. The pulses help a heart beat at the right speed. Pacemakers have saved many lives. Today pacemaker data can even be uploaded to the Internet. Doctors can see a heart's condition in real time.

Bioengineering is much more than creating machines. Engineers also create organs from scratch. The organs are made of real human tissue. This technology will revolutionize transplants. Organs grown from a

IN THE REAL WORLD
Growing a Heart

Growing a real organ is no easy task. Organs can have dozens of types of cells that need to work together. For bioengineers, getting the cells to work is just the beginning. The cells must then be grown to function in the shape of a heart.

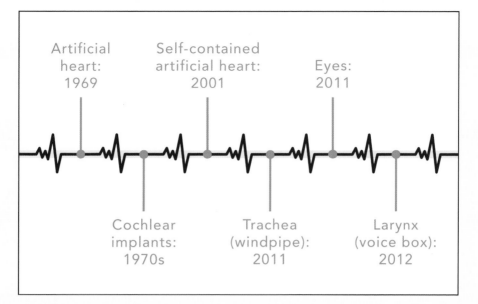

Artificial Organs

The quest for artificial organs is about more than just new hearts. Above is a timeline of some of the artificial organs that have been implanted into human bodies. Which organs seem to be missing? Which might be in highest demand?

patient's cells may work well inside a person's body. Also, transplant organs are in short supply. Building new ones would eliminate long waits on transplant lists.

Bioengineers improve people's lives. Sometimes they use devices inside the body. Sometimes they build new limbs. They work with living tissue to grow new organs.

Corn is one of many crops that has been touched by bioengineering.

Bioengineers are not focused only on medicine. They also work in other fields, such as agriculture. Their research is changing the way we grow our food. Bioengineering helps build a world where people live longer, healthier lives.

EXPLORE ONLINE

Chapter One discusses some of the achievements of bioengineers. The website below shows many of the challenges they have overcome. What new information did you learn from the website? How was information there presented differently from in Chapter One?

Want To Be a Bioengineer?
mycorelibrary.com/bioengineering

CHAPTER TWO

RECREATING THE BODY

With its amazing technology, bioengineering might seem like a new field. However, its history goes back thousands of years. The first person who built a walking stick was doing an early form of bioengineering. From walking sticks to artificial legs, bioengineering has come a long way.

Advanced technology allows bioengineers to build functional replacement parts for the body.

The First Wheelchair

Wheelchairs are an early example of bioengineering. However, the first ones were not made as medical devices. In 1595 King Philip II of Spain had a throne on wheels. It was designed for comfort rather than mobility. But wheelchairs began being used to move around just decades later. And by 1655, a Flemish watchmaker had made the first wheelchair the user could move. The person could move by turning a crank rather than being pushed.

Early Bioengineering

One of the first feats of bioengineering was a prosthetic big toe. Found in the tomb of an Egyptian noblewoman, it is thought to date to approximately 950 BCE. The wooden toe was created to be lifelike. It is even carved with a toenail. But the toe was functional too. It was fitted to the foot with leather straps. The toe made it easier to walk.

War injuries led to more advanced prostheses. Roman general Marcus Sergius lost his right hand in battle in the 200s BCE. However, he wanted to rejoin the fight. He had a new hand made. This hand was

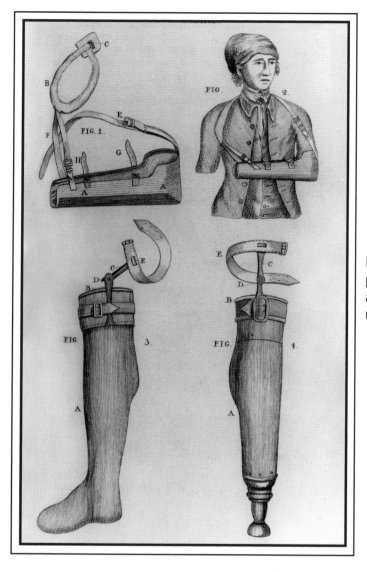

Many early prosthetic arms and legs were made of wood.

made of iron. The fingers were curled so he could hold a shield. Thanks to the prosthesis, he could keep fighting.

Early hearing aids were simple horn-shaped devices.

As time went on, artificial limbs became more complex. In 1504 a German soldier had his right arm damaged by a cannonball. His prosthetic arm was impressive. Unlike Sergius's hand, his arm and fingers could move. He could even hold a quill pen.

Later Developments

Bioengineering was not just about replacing lost limbs. Other devices were used to improve quality of life. One such invention was the hearing aid. Early hearing aids came in the form of ear trumpets. These devices were shaped like a funnel. The narrow end was placed near or in the ear. Then the wide end gathered sound. Ear trumpets made sounds a bit louder. But they did not help in cases of extreme hearing loss.

In the early 1900s, hearing aids saw big improvements. Inventors such as Thomas Edison created electric aids that could be carried around. Parts of a recent invention, the telephone, were used in these devices.

The Iron Lung

In the early 1900s, the disease polio killed many people. It paralyzed the lungs. Patients found it hard or impossible to breathe. Researchers looked for ways to keep a person breathing. They developed the iron lung. An iron lung is a sealed box. Most of the patient's body is placed inside its metal casing. Only the head sticks out. The chamber is sealed, and air pressure forces the lungs to expand and contract. This helps the person continue to breathe.

By the mid-1900s, technology was evolving rapidly. Computers made it possible to build smaller, better devices. Bioengineers took advantage of these advances. Medicine was about to change forever.

Information about Marcus Sergius comes from the writings of historian Pliny the Elder. In *Natural History*, Pliny writes:

> *Nobody—at least in my opinion—can rightly rank any man above Marcus Sergius. . . . In his second campaign Sergius lost his right hand. In two campaigns he was wounded twenty-three times, with the result that he had no use in either hand or either foot: only his spirit remained intact. Although disabled, Sergius served in many subsequent campaigns. He was twice captured by Hannibal—no ordinary foe—from whom twice he escaped, although kept in chains and shackles every day for twenty months. He fought four times with only his left hand, while two horses he was riding were stabbed beneath him.*
>
> *He had a right hand made of iron for him and, going into battle with this bound to his arm, raised the siege of Cremona, saved Placentia and captured twelve enemy camps in Gaul.*
>
> *Source: Pliny the Elder. "Pliny's Natural History." Archive.org. Archive.org, n.d. Web. July 7, 2015.*

Consider Your Audience

Adapt this passage for a different audience, such as your principal or friends. How does your version differ from the original text and why?

CHAPTER THREE

CAREER PATHS

Bioengineers work in many different fields. One major area is prosthetics. Prostheses have come a long way since the wooden toe of ancient Egypt. Today they are made of durable metals and plastics. And these limbs are more than just replacement parts. Bioengineers have created arms full of electrical circuits that act like nerves. Sensors in the arm send information along wires.

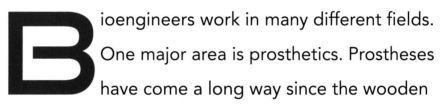

Bioengineers are working to improve lives through the invention of prosthetic limbs and other devices.

The wires connect to nerve endings. The nerves send information to the brain. This lets people feel what they are touching.

Inside the Body

Some bioengineers work on devices that go inside the body. These include pacemakers and hip replacements. One device has allowed bioengineers to change the way they approach hearing loss. It is called the cochlear implant. The cochlea is a part of the ear. Cochlear implants do not amplify sound, as hearing aids do. They turn vibrations from sound into electronic signals. Then they send these signals to the brain. The implants allow

Cochlear Controversy

Cochlear implants improve hearing, but some members of the deaf community oppose them. Some feel the implant suggests a deaf person is broken and needs to be fixed. Others worry the implants might erase deaf culture. Sign language might become a thing of the past. People argue a deaf person would become completely reliant on the implant.

Cochlear implants include parts both inside and outside the body.

R

Hip replacements must be made out of materials that
will be safe within the body for decades.

the user to hear human speech, but they are not as sensitive as a real cochlea. Bioengineers are working on ways to improve them.

To improve or invent devices, bioengineers need the right materials. Finding them can be a challenging task. Many materials have negative effects on the human body. Some implants need to stay within a person's body for many years. The materials must be safe for human use. One way to do this is to use real human tissue. Implants may get more and more like the parts they are replacing.

Working on a Small Scale

Bioengineering is not just about making artificial arms or legs. Researchers in the field also engineer at cellular levels. Cells are the tiny building blocks of living things. Scientists want to understand how they work together to do their jobs. For example, researchers are looking into how heart cells beat. They also want to learn how cells respond to major illnesses or injuries. This could let bioengineers make cells that help the body recover. Knowing how cells work also helps engineers build devices that work well with the body.

Some bioengineers work with even smaller things. They deal with nanotechnology. This field involves tiny devices that move through the bloodstream. These little machines could help scientists understand how medicine works in the body. This is important for medicines that need to target a specific organ, such as the kidneys.

Work Outside the Body

Bioengineers work outside the medical field

Nanotechnology may one day make it possible for scientists to build tiny machines that work on individual cells in the body.

Golden rice, *left*, is one of many foods made possible by genetic engineering.

as well. Some work in agriculture. They breed crops to improve them. Engineers may add nutrients or make crops more resistant to insects. They may also genetically modify the crop to achieve these changes. For example, bioengineers have added vitamin A to a type of rice. This turned the rice a yellow color. It was given the name Golden Rice. A lack of vitamin A can lead to eyesight trouble and other health issues. Golden Rice can prevent these problems.

Bioengineers may be responsible for many aspects of food safety. They might create devices to monitor food products. They may check genetically modified foods for safety. Understanding the consequences of genetic changes is the job of bioengineers.

Becoming a Bioengineer

Bioengineering is one of the fastest growing careers. However, the overall number of jobs in the field is still small. Only about 3 percent of engineers are bioengineers. This makes bioengineering a

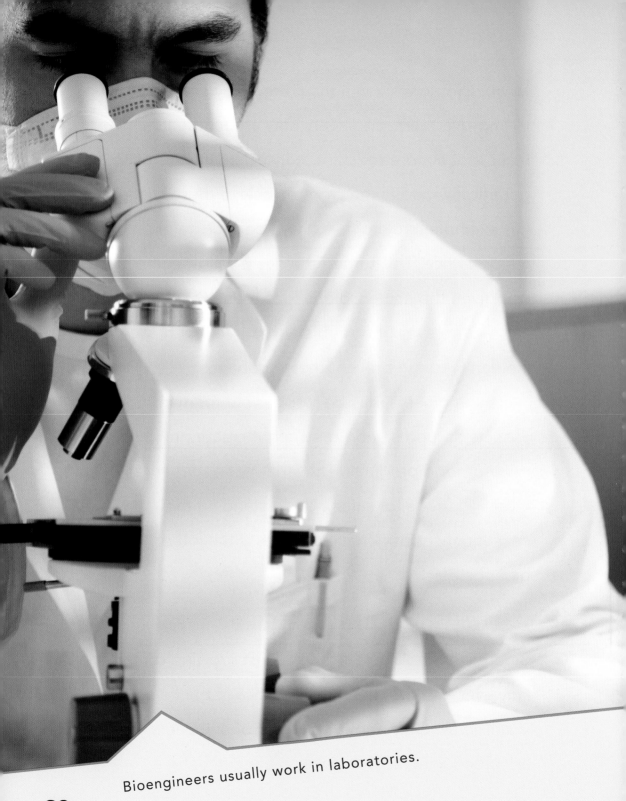

Bioengineers usually work in laboratories.

competitive area. Students should go to colleges with strong engineering and biology programs. Doing research or an internship in college is a great way to get into the industry.

Bioengineers can become doctors or university researchers. Others may work at medical device companies. The average salary for a bioengineer in 2014 was more than $90,000.

FURTHER EVIDENCE

This chapter is about what bioengineers do. What are the main points given in the chapter? Read the article below. Does it support the chapter? Does it give more evidence?

Bioengineering and Health Care

mycorelibrary.com/bioengineering

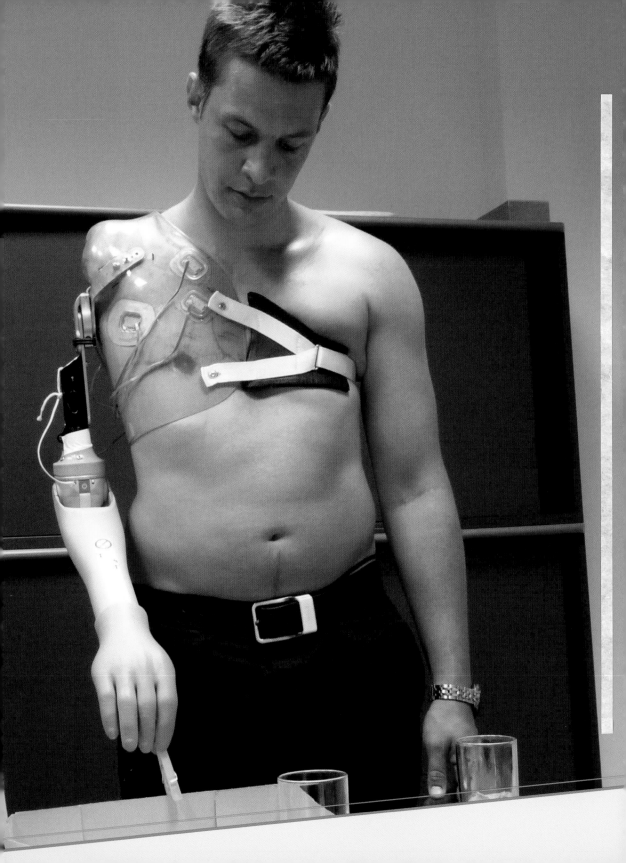

CHAPTER 4

DESIGNING THE FUTURE

The products of bioengineering may seem like science fiction. Bioengineers create artificial arms, ears, and hearts. They modify the genetics of food. These researchers use technology to help people stay healthier and live longer. In the future, they will push the boundaries of science even further.

New prosthetic arms let patients touch and feel objects around them.

Catching Problems Before They Start

One major goal is to create machines that are better at diagnosis. Today, most devices are used after an illness begins. New machines could catch diseases earlier than is currently possible.

One example is a new scan that might be able to detect Alzheimer's disease. This disease affects a person's memory. A person with advanced Alzheimer's may not know who or where they are. With the new scan, an MRI machine is used to look for changes in the brain. It examines the part of the brain where memory is stored. If there are changes in that area, it might indicate that Alzheimer's is present.

Creating Transplants

Scientists cannot yet grow a full organ from scratch. However, they are getting closer. Bioengineers are developing bioartificial transplants. As the name suggests, they are part biological and part artificial. A scaffold is made out of plastic. This scaffold is

New scans may make it possible to catch diseases earlier than ever before.

Engineers can use three-dimensional printers to build scaffolds for organs.

like a framework upon which cells can grow. Then researchers can take cells from the person who needs the transplant. Those cells are added to the scaffold. The cells grow around the scaffold. The result is a new organ that can be implanted.

Since the new organ is made out of the person's own cells, the chance of the transplant working is much higher. This is a major breakthrough. It also means a person would not have to wait for an organ donor. Organs could be made specifically for individual patients.

Stem Cells

In order to make transplant organs, scientists use stem cells. These cells are capable of turning into any cell in the body. The body can send them a signal asking for a certain type of cell. Scientists are researching how to trigger these signals in the lab.

Ethical Issues

Bioengineering offers many new ways to keep people healthy. However, some people are concerned about the direction it is heading. They debate the future

A Child with Three Parents

In early 2015, the British government approved something that may sound impossible: a child with three parents. The plan was a response to a specific birth defect. Some mothers pass down faulty mitochondria to their children. These parts of cells produce energy that lets the cell function. Bioengineers realized they could take the mitochondria from a healthy woman and add them to the baby's genes. This third parent would only contribute approximately 0.01% of the child's genes.

of genetic engineering. Genetic engineering is when DNA is modified to accomplish a goal. DNA holds all the information about an organism's genes. Genes produce an organism's characteristics, such as eye and hair color. People imagine a future in which parents can change their baby's genes before it is born. They could stop it from getting diseases. They could also change eye or hair color.

These might not seem like a big deal. For solving medical problems, genetic engineering actually

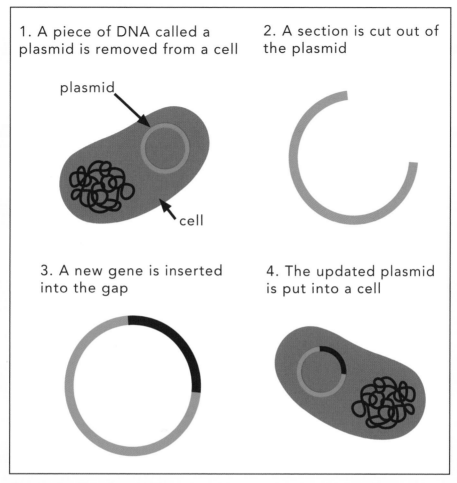

1. A piece of DNA called a plasmid is removed from a cell

plasmid

cell

2. A section is cut out of the plasmid

3. A new gene is inserted into the gap

4. The updated plasmid is put into a cell

Genetic Engineering

One method of genetic engineering involves four major steps. Take a look at the infographic above. How might this technology be used to improve human health? Why might some people see genetic engineering as a controversial science?

looks like a good thing. But there are concerns about equality. Would only the rich have access to such technology? Or would it be available for everyone?

Who would be in charge of regulating it? Would picking genes mean our destiny is set before we're even born?

These are important questions. Bioengineers must think about these kinds of issues. As with all scientific advances, bioengineering can make a huge impact on society. Understanding the ethics of this technology will be part of a bioengineer's job.

Cloning is the process of making a genetic copy of an organism. The following passage discusses the controversy around cloning and genetic engineering:

> *Some say cloning is wrong because it violates the right to autonomy: by choosing a child's genetic makeup in advance, parents deny the child's right to an open future. A similar objection can be raised against any form of bioengineering that allows parents to select or reject genetic characteristics. According to this argument, genetic enhancements for musical talent, say, or athletic prowess, would point children toward particular choices, and so designer children would never be fully free. . . . The moral quandary arises when people use such therapy not to cure a disease but to reach beyond health, to enhance their physical or cognitive capacities, to lift themselves above the norm.*
>
> Source: Michael J. Sandel. "The Case Against Perfection." The Atlantic. *The Atlantic, April 2004. Web. July 7, 2015.*

The Big Idea

Read the text carefully. What is the main idea? What details did the author use to support the main idea? Why are people opposed to genetic modification and cloning? Why might they be in favor of it?

- The history of bioengineering goes back thousands of years.

- Bioengineers must know about both biological systems and technology.

- Careers in bioengineering could involve creating new prostheses or implants.

- Other careers could involve understanding how cells work.

- Bioengineers also help hospitals maintain important medical devices.

- Bioengineering includes both large-scale objects, such as artificial legs and arms, and small-scale objects, such as the tiny machines in the field of nanotechnology.

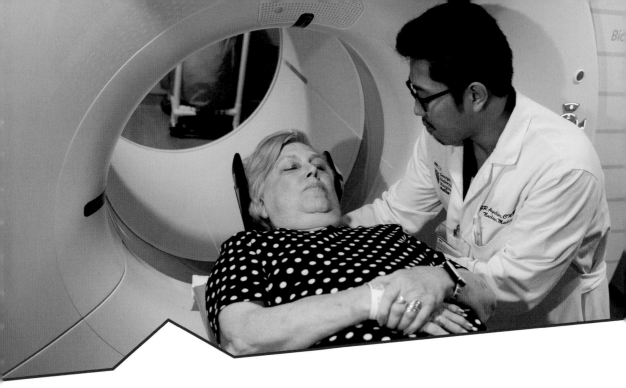

- Some bioengineers work to genetically modify crops.

- The future of bioengineering will have to consider the many ethical consequences of having more control over the human body.

STOP AND THINK

Say What?

Reading about biotechnology and science might mean learning a lot of new vocabulary. Find five words in this book that you've never heard before. Use a dictionary to find out what they mean. Then write the meanings in your own words, and use each word in a new sentence.

Why Do I Care?

Maybe you do not have interest in bioengineering. But that does not mean bioengineering does not impact your world. Write a short essay on how bioengineering could affect your life or the lives of those you care about. What about the lives of others in the world?

Surprise Me

Chapter Three describes many job roles a bioengineer may have. After reading this book, what two or three facts about bioengineers and their work did you find most surprising? Write a few sentences about each fact. Why did you find each fact surprising?

You Are There

This book discusses the very first artificial heart. Imagine you were around in the 1960s and witnessed the artificial heart firsthand. Write a letter home to your friends about this amazing new piece of technology. What is it like to see an artificial organ? Be sure to add plenty of detail to your notes.

GLOSSARY

bioartificial
something that is made of
both biological and artificial
materials

MRI machine
a machine that uses magnetic
fields to create images of the
inside of the body

circuit
a group of wiring through
which electricity can flow

nanotechnology
technology that works with
devices smaller than 100
micrometers (0.003 inches)

diagnosis
identifying an illness

prosthesis
an artificial part of the body

genetic engineering
modifications made to genes
and DNA

transplant
an operation in which a new
organ is placed in the body

LEARN MORE

Books

Abramovitz, Melissa. *Amazing Feats of Biological Engineering*. Minneapolis: Abdo Publishing, 2014.

Walker, Richard. *Human Body*. New York: DK, 2014.

Websites

To learn more about STEM in the Real World, visit **booklinks.abdopublishing.com.** These links are routinely monitored and updated to provide the most current information available.

Visit **mycorelibrary.com** for free additional tools for teachers and students.

INDEX

ABOUT THE AUTHOR

Meg Marquardt has a bachelor's degree in physics and a master's degree in science journalism. She lives in Omaha, Nebraska, with her two science-minded cats, Lagrange and Doppler.